GRADE 3 GRAMMAR 1

Fun-filled Activities

An imprint of Om Books International

Sentence

A sentence is a group of words that makes a complete thought.

For example:

Linda looked at the huge building.

Put a tick on the group of words that make a sentence and cross on the ones that don't.

1. John's family has moved to a new city.
2. Wants to go to a new school.
3. John is worried about his first day at school.
4. Makes a list of things.
5. Feels nervous.
6. His father drove him to the school.
7. He sits quietly in the car.
8. Sees huge building of the school.
9. Then he saw his new classroom.
10. Talked to everyone and made friends.

How was your first day at school? Write 5 sentences about it.

____

____

____

____

____

____

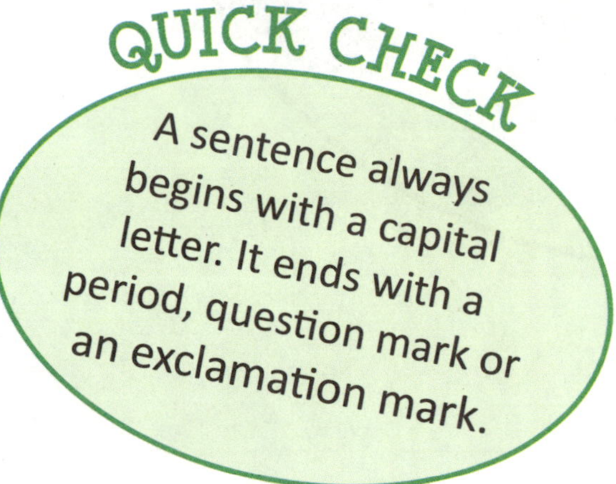

Statement And Question

A statement is a sentence that tells something. It ends with a period.

Example: There are seven cookies left in the jar.

A question is a sentence that asks something. It ends with a question mark.

Example: How many cookies are left in the jar?

Read the sentences below. Write S if it is a statement and Q if it is a question.

1. Mr Crow has a beautiful sunflower garden. ☐
2. Do you know what he first does to plant the flowers? ☐
3. He digs many holes in the soil. ☐
4. It is not an easy task to do. ☐
5. He then places a seed carefully in each hole. ☐
6. What do these seeds need to grow? ☐
7. They need plenty of sunlight and water. ☐
8. The seedlings sprout after a few days. ☐
9. The plants grow tall and flowers bloom. ☐
10. Would you like to grow sunflowers too? ☐

Statement And Question

Rearrange the words to make meaningful sentences. Use capital letters and end marks correctly.

1. a map is earth on a flat a drawing of paper
2. way and locate us to find our It helps places
3. do how to use you know a map
4. a key that helps map has a us understand it
5. symbols that the key has are used in a map
6. symbols on the map and can you see directions
7. able will you this map use be to

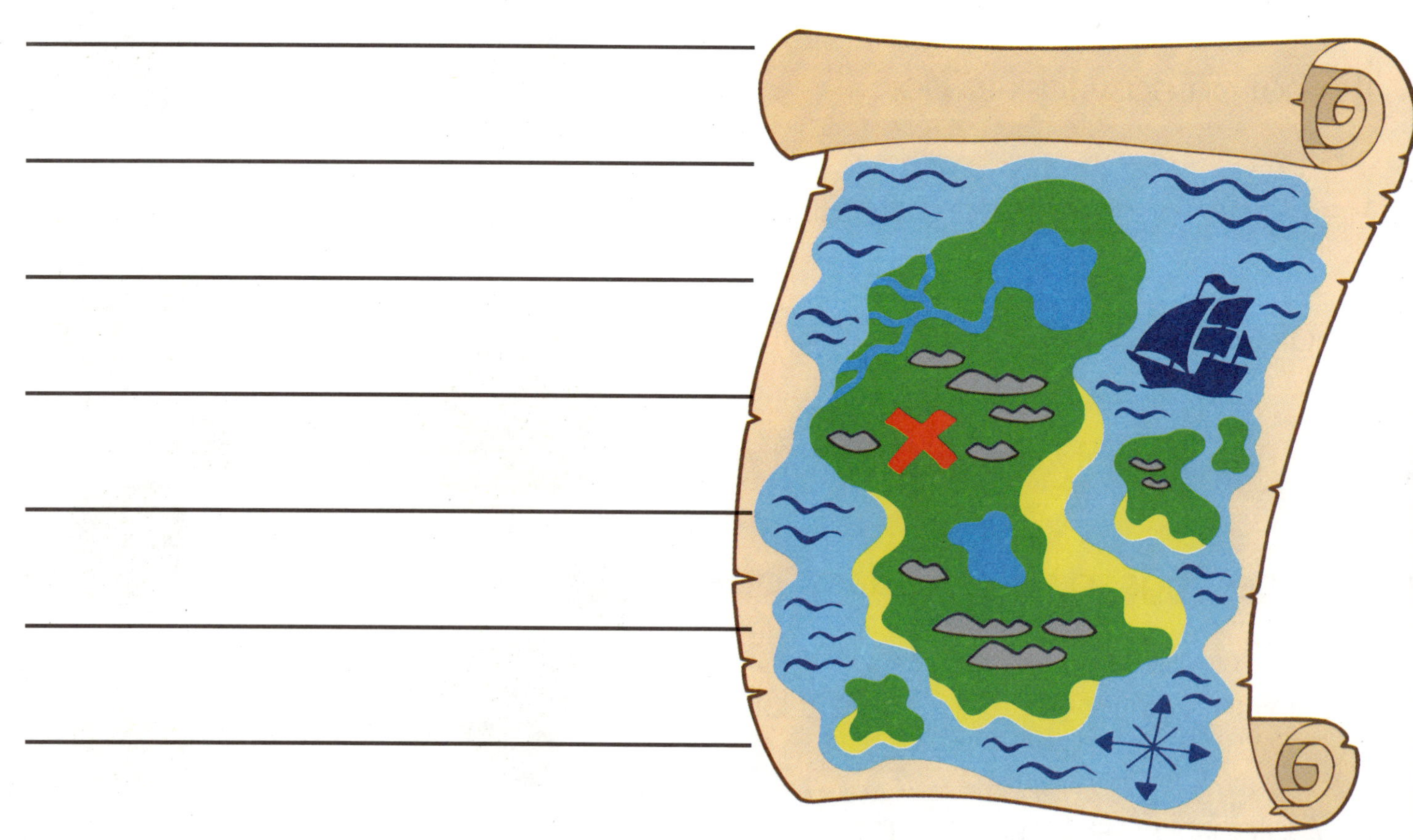

Try it! Use the word dance to make a statement and a question.

Command And Exclamation

A command is a sentence that tells or asks someone to do something. It ends with a period. The word you is understood so we don't write you.

Example:
Post the letter today.

An exclamation shows strong feeling. It ends with an exclamation mark (!)
Example: Here's a wonderful gift for you!

After each sentence, write C for command and E for exclamation for the kind of sentence it is. Then write the sentence correctly. Use capital letters and end marks.

1. remember to write to uncle james

   ____

2. oh, I really forgot about that

   ____

3. whew, I'm glad you reminded me

   ____

4. thank him for the amazing book he sent

   ____

5. hand me that envelope

   ____

6. hey, I'll send him my new bike picture

   ____

7. that's a wonderful idea

   ____

8. write a note on the picture for him

   ____

Identifying Types Of Sentences

Read each sentence and write the ending punctuation in the box. Also write the kind of sentence it is.

1. A spider is not an insect ☐ ____________
2. Wow they are amazing creatures ☐ ____________
3. Spiders can have two, five or even eight eyes ☐ ____________
4. Can all spiders spin silk ☐ ____________

5. It's amazing that they don't stick to their web ☐ ____________
6. Spiders eat insects ☐ ____________
7. Where do spiders live ☐ ____________
8. Do not tear spider webs ☐ ____________

Sentences

Kind of sentence	What the sentence does	Ending punctuation
Statement	tells you something	.
Command	tells you to do something	.
Question	asks something	?
Exclamation	shows strong feelings	!

Types Of Sentences

Identify the type of sentence. Put the correct punctuation mark for each sentence.

QUICK CHECK

Both commands and statements end in a period.

1. An ice cream is a frozen dessert made of cream, flavours and sweeteners
2. Do you know who first made ice cream
3. The first frozen dessert is credited to Emperor Nero of Rome
4. What was the first ice cream made of
5. It was a mixture of snow, nectar, fruit pulp and honey
6. Give me a scoop of ice cream
7. Wow it's really yummy
8. May I have some more please
9. Eat the ice cream before it melts
10. What a delicious treat it was

Subject And Predicate

A sentence has two parts- subject and predicate.
The subject of the sentence is whom or what the sentence is about.
The predicate of a sentence tells what the subject does or is.

Example:
Sentence: The children are going on a trip to hills.
Subject: The children
Predicate: are going on a trip to hills

Circle the subject and underline the predicate in each sentence.

1. The students of Grade 3 are going to the art museum.
2. They all board the bus at 9 am.
3. They see huge buildings on the way.
4. Jim and Kelly are very excited to go there.
5. Kelly loves to draw.
6. Her favourite painter is Van Gogh.
7. The children see wonderful paintings of different painters.
8. They had a nice day at the museum.

Try it!

Write as many subjects as you can for the predicate given below.

________________________ are yummy and sweet to taste.

Subject And Predicate

Read each group of words given below. Write S for subject and P for predicate.

☐ ants	☐ are three different kinds of ants
☐ there	☐ worker
☐ spends her life laying eggs	☐ build chambers in their colony to store food
☐ builds the mound and supplies the colony with food	☐ are social insects
☐ ants	☐ the queen

Now combine each subject with a predicate and form a complete sentence. Write them below.

1. ______________________________

2. ______________________________

3. ______________________________

4. ______________________________

5. ______________________________

Subject And Predicate

Complete the sentences by writing a suitable subject or predicate.

1. Jacob ______________________________.
2. ____________ has been a favourite lunch spot for years.
3. Some people eat __________________.
4. ____________ eat there even more often.
5. ____________ is the topping people like the most.
6. Tomatoes are not __________________.
7. Jacob's burgers ________________.
8. ____________ will make them anyway you want.
9. ________________________ cold drink and chips too.
10. You should __________________.

Nouns

Read the word on each brick. Decide if the word is a noun. If it is a noun, circle the box. If it is not, leave it uncircled.

Try it!

Write any ten nouns related to a garden.

Proper And Common Nouns

A common noun names any person, place, animal or thing.
Example: actor, garden
A proper noun names a special person, place, animal or thing.
Example: Mr Clark, Neo Street, Monday

QUICK CHECK
A proper noun always begins with a capital letter.

Write common or proper for the underlined words to identify the type of nouns they are.

1. Our class went on a trip to the <u>New Land Museum.</u> __________
2. We saw models of different <u>habitats</u> there. __________
3. The <u>teacher</u> took us to see photographs of various animals. __________
4. We saw a show about <u>insects.</u> __________
5. I liked <u>spiders</u> the most. __________
6. <u>Molly</u> liked the bees most. __________
7. There were also huge models of <u>dinosaurs.</u> __________
8. We all wrote our notes in the <u>journal.</u> __________
9. Robert knows a lot about <u>rainforests.</u> __________
10. It is amazing to know about <u>nature.</u> __________

Try it! Write 5-7 lines on your favourite animal. Identify the common and proper nouns.

Proper And Common Nouns

Circle the nouns using a pencil. Then underline each noun using the colour code.

1. Today is a busy day at the Big Motors.
2. Many people have come to buy vehicles.
3. Mr Peter is looking at a truck.
4. His brother wants to buy a red motorcycle.
5. There is a woman looking at the van.
6. A grocer wants to drive the car in the city.
7. The salespersons are guiding the customers.
8. The blue car is the costliest of all.
9. The farmer wants a truck to drive to his farm.
10. Every buyer is looking for a discount.

Proper nouns- blue
Common nouns- green

Try it!

Use any 3 nouns from this page and make a sentence.

Proper And Common Nouns

Write each sentence using capital letters for proper nouns.

1. it was very hot on sunday afternoon.

____

2. mac and kiara sat on the garden bench.

____

3. mac was munching on chocolate cookies.

____

4. kiara was looking at the garden weeds.

____

5. mac put his cookie on the bench and joined her.

____

6. a group of ants swarmed around the cookies!

____

7. mac was amazed to see the tiny creatures together.

____

8. kiara ran inside and got a magnifying glass.

____

9. the children saw how the ants worked together.

____

10. mac and kiara saw more ants every evening.

____

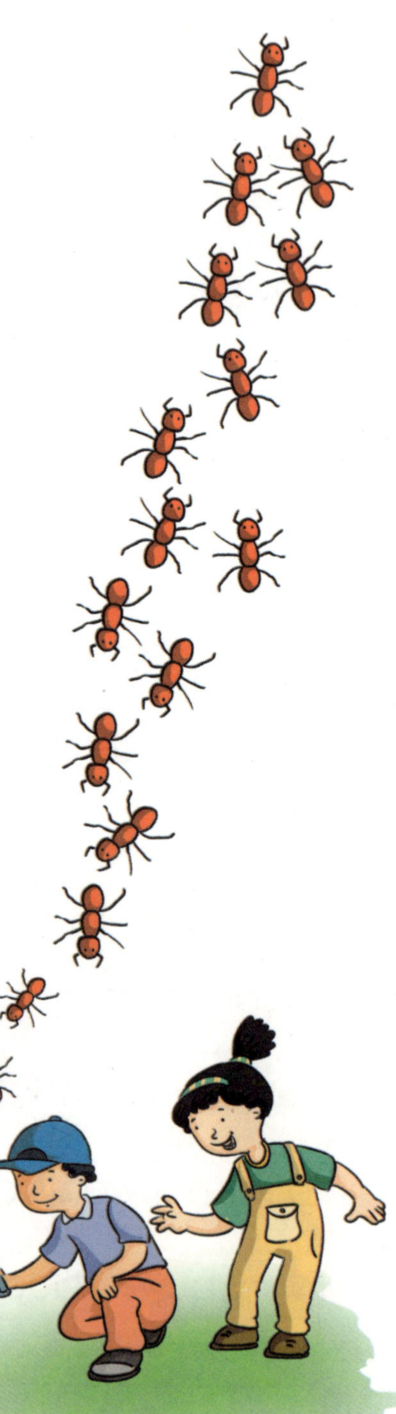

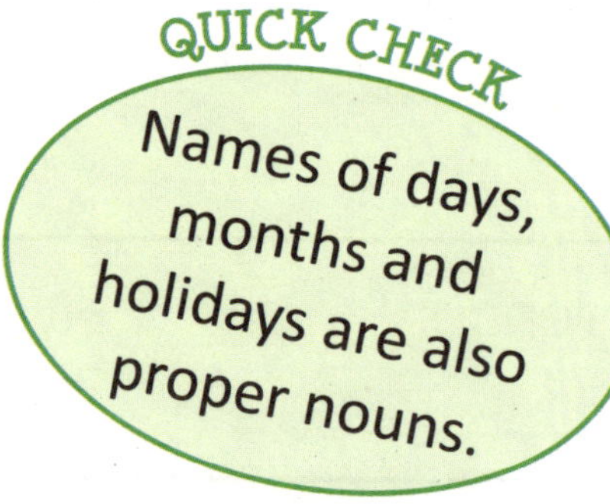

Abstract Nouns

Abstract nouns name feelings and things we cannot see or touch.
Example: I can feel the warmth of the sun.

Circle the abstract nouns from the words given below.

Monday, happiness, second, doctor, strength, friendship, love, wish, wheels, perfume, pepper, book, fragrance, speed

Use these abstract nouns to make sentences of your own.

1. Flavour-
2. Worry-
3. Honesty-
4. Depth

Collective Nouns

A collective noun is the name given to a group.

Find the collective nouns in the grid and fill in the blanks.

P	T	E	A	M	C	A	B	R	W
A	C	R	E	W	G	R	P	D	S
R	B	B	C	U	T	M	S	L	M
L	O	E	O	D	H	Y	R	Y	F
I	W	E	G	U	S	H	O	R	P
A	L	G	C	G	Q	A	J	X	A
M	F	W	B	L	B	U	J	I	C
E	B	A	A	D	A	L	E	G	K
N	G	D	N	Q	G	S	N	T	E
T	X	R	D	N	I	I	S	K	T

1. A ____________ of students.
2. An ____________ of soldiers.
3. A ____________ of sailors.
4. A ____________ of musicians.
5. A ____________ of fish.
6. A ____________ of owls
7. A ____________ of players.
8. A ____________ of flowers.
9. A ____________ of rice.
10. A ____________ of cards.

Possessive Nouns

A possessive noun is a noun that shows who or what owns or has something.

We add an **apostrophe (')** and an **s** to a singular noun to make it possessive.
We add an **apostrophe (')** to make most plural nouns possessive.
We add an **apostrophe (')** and an **s** to form the possessive of plural nouns that do not end in **s.**

Example: Bruno's boat, students' notebooks, children's park

Patrick and his friends forgot some winter items near the skating rink.
Use a possessive noun to show to whom each item belongs.

Possessive Nouns

Complete each sentence with the possessive form of the noun in brackets.

1. (Miss Martha) _______________ bag has a big poster in it.
2. The children saw that it was about the (Earth) ___________solar system.
3. Miss Martha explained that the (planets) ___________paths around the Sun are called orbits.
4. The (orbits) ________________lengths are all different.
5. A (comet)_______________ tail is made of dust and gas.
6. Miss Martha answered the (children) _______________questions.
7. The (Sun) ___________rays take eight minutes to reach us.
8. (Jupiter) ____________ size is greater than that of Earth.
9. "What are (Saturn) _________________rings made of?" asked Neo.
10. "Is that (Moon)__________ light?"

Action Verbs

An action verb is a word that shows action.
An action verb tells what the subject of the sentence does.

Example: Martha cooks delicious food.

James talks to his friends.

Read the sentences and circle the action verbs.

1. I like the day after Thanksgiving.
2. We celebrate this day every year in a grand manner.
3. Father gets up early, goes to the kitchen and cooks.
4. He takes the vegetables and uses them for soup.
5. He then carves the turkey.
6. The next is to cut the vegetables and heat the water.
7. Later we eat a delicious meal.
8. Patrick loves the soup that father makes.
9. He also eats plenty of cranberries stuffing and pie.
10. Everybody enjoys this special day.

Try it! Write 5 action verbs related to kitchen and make sentences with them.

Present Tense Verbs

A verb in the present tense tells what happens now. A present tense verb must agree with its subject.

We add -s to most verbs if the subject is singular. We do not add -s or -es to a present-tense verb when the subject is plural or I or you.

Example: Kelly plays badminton every day.
The girls play badminton every day.

QUICK CHECK

The tense of a verb tells us the time at which the action happens. Verbs can be written in present, past and future tense.

Complete each sentence using the action verbs in the present tense.

1. We _________ (go, goes) to the garden every day.
2. I __________ (want, wants) to pull all the weeds.
3. Kim ______________ (come, comes) to pick flowers.
4. Molly __________(pick, picks) a rose and _______ (give, gives) to her mother.
5. Kim and Molly ____________ (see, sees) many rosebushes.
6. Bees come and ___________(collect, collects) pollen from the flowers.
7. Jenny _________(find, finds) a ladybug near the bushes.
8. We ___________(work, works) in the garden and have fun.

Past Tense

A verb in the past tense tells about an action that has already happened. We add -ed to most verbs to show past tense.

Example: We walked to the beach.

Find the past-tense verb in each sentence. Circle it.

1. Polly's family reached the beach in the morning.
2. They placed their towels on the sand.
3. Polly's brother picked up the buckets.
4. He filled Polly's bucket with sand.
5. Father stacked the buckets of sand. .
6. The children formed towers at each corner.
7. They shaped a big square of sand in the centre.
8. Everyone liked the size of the castle.
9. The children splashed in the water happily.
10. They played for many hours and had fun.

Try it!

Write 3 sentences to tell what you did last Sunday.

____

____

____

____

____

____

____

____

____

Past Tense

Write the past tense form of each word on the blank.

Spelling rules
1. Just add **–ed.**
2. Drop the final **e** and add **–ed.**
3. Double the final consonant and add **–ed.**
4. Change the **y** after a consonant to i and add **–ed.**

Past Tense

Fill in the blanks with the past tense of the verbs in the brackets.

1. Alicia ______________ (visit) a bowling alley.

2. A pro ____________ (help) Alicia.

3. She ___________(follow) the pro's advice.

4. She ___________(practice) hard.

5. The other bowlers ___________(roll) heavy balls.

6. A bowler ______________(aim) his ball carefully.

7. The ball ______________(hit) the pins.

8. Some bowlers ___________ (talk) to Alicia.

9. They _____________(guide) her with some tips.

10. Alicia _______________(bowl) two strikes in one game.

QUICK CHECK

Some verbs don't change in the past tense. Example: put, cut, hit.

Irregular Past Verbs

Some action verbs change completely in the past tense.

Example: catch-caught, go-went.

Fill in the balloons with the past form of the action verbs.

Past Tense

Correct the sentences by changing the underlined verbs to the past tense.

1. The bird flap its wings through the air and turn towards the shore.

____

2. It drift through the sky slowly and land on a rock.

____

3. The bird jump to another rock, pick up a piece of bread and swallow it.

____

4. The bird find a candy wrapper, a pretzel and a few bugs.

____

5. It poke, pull and rip apart the wrapper.

____

6. Then the bird fly into the clear, bright, blue sky.

____

Future Tense

A verb in the future tense tells about an action that is going to happen. To write about the future, use the special verb 'will'.

Example:
Sam will paint a picture in the evening.

Read the sentences and circle the verb that is in future tense.

1. Roger will climb the Rocky Ridge next week.
2. He will buy new shoes.
3. Roger will use his own shoes.
4. He will need a new helmet.
5. Roger's friend Pam will also go with him.
6. Roger will help his friend Pam to climb.
7. He will tell Pam about the trail.
8. The friends will have a great time today.

Try it!

What will happen when Roger reaches the ridge, puts on his helmet and starts climbing?

Write a few sentences about it in the future tense.

Future Tense

Complete the sentences by changing the verbs into future tense.

1. Bonnie ______________ (go) to the Maldives tomorrow.
2. She will __________(pack) all her baggage tonight.
3. The next morning, she __________(lock) all the doors of her house.
4. She _____________(reach) the airport at 5:00 pm.
5. Bonnie ___________(locate) her airline.
6. She __________ (need) to go to the departure terminal.
7. Bonnie __________ (show) her boarding pass to the attendant.
8. The security personnel ___________(check) her luggage.
9. She ___________(leave) behind metal objects if any.
10. Then Bonnie ___________(board) the plane.

Try it!

What are your plans for the next travel? Write 8 sentences to describe your plans. Do you remember you have to use the future tense?

____

____

____

____

____

____

____

____

____

Verbs Be, Do And Have

The verbs be, do, and have all have special forms in the present tense. The chart shows which form to use with a given subject.

Subject	Be	Do	Have
I	am	do	have
he, she, it	is	does	has
we, you, they	are	do	have

Write the correct form of verbs in the blanks.

1. Maria _________ our favourite baker.

2. We _________ big fans of her strawberry pie.

3. They _________ the best pies in the world.

4. I ________ sure you will like them.

5. You ________ never hungry when you leave her bakery.

6. Maria __________ a lot of work to pick strawberries.

7. Liza __________ not like strawberries.

8. We also _________ many strawberry plants in our garden.

9. The gardener _________ to pick the strawberries tomorrow.

10. These strawberries _________ the most delicious flavour.

Verbs Be, Do And Have

The verbs be, do, and have all have special forms in the past tense. The chart shows which form to use with a given subject.

Subject	Be	Do	Have
I	was	did	had
he, she, it	was	did	had
we, you, they	were	did	had

Fill in the blanks with the past form of be, do and have.

1. Last week we ___________ a report on apple farming.
2. I _________ happy to talk about my favourite fruit.
3. All the students ________ a lot of research.
4. They __________ excited to read a lot of information.
5. Robert _______ to study a lot.
6. He __________ not aware of apple farming.
7. Liza and Pam _________ the first to complete the report.
8. The teacher ______ happy to see our charts.

Answer Key

Page 2

1
3
6
7
9 are sentences

Page 3

1. This is Mr. Crow's beautiful sunflower garden. S
2. Do you know what he first does to plant the flowers? Q
3. He digs many holes in the soil. S
4. It is not an easy task to do. S
5. He then places a seed carefully in each hole. S
6. What do these seeds need to grow? Q
7. They need plenty of sunlight and water. S
8. The seedlings sprout after a few days. S
9. The plants grow tall and flowers bloom. S
10. Would you like to grow sunflowers too? Q

Page 4

1 A map is a flag drawing of earth on paper.
2 It helps us to find places and locate our way.
3 Do you know how to use a map?
4 A map has a key that helps us understand it.
5 A key has symbols that are used in a map.
6 Can you see symbols and directions on the map?
7 Will you be able to use this map?

Page 5

Children will write the sentences using punctuation marks on their own.

The kind of sentences are-

1. C
2. E.
3. E.
4. C.
5. C.
6. E.
7. E.
8. C

Page 6

1. Statement
2. Exclamation
3. Statement
4. Question
5. Exclamation
6. Statement
7. Question
8. Statement

Page 7

1. Statement- put a period
2. Question- put a question mark
3. Statement- put a period
4. Question- put a question mark
5. Statement- put a period
6. Statement- put a period
7. Exclamation - put an exclamation mark
8. Question- put a question mark
9. Statement- put a period
10. Exclamation- put an exclamation mark

Page 8

1. The students of Grade 3 are going to the art museum.
2. They all board the bus at 9 am.
3. They see huge buildings on the way.
4. Jim and Kelly are very excited to go there.
5. Kelly loves to draw.
6. Her favourite painter is Van Gogh.
7. The children see wonderful paintings of different painters.
8. They had a nice day at the museum.

Page 9

Children will join sentences on their own.

Page 10

Children will write subjects and predicates on their own.

Page 11

The words given below are nouns.

screwdriver, engineer, Mall Street, mason, gardener, bush, worker, toolkit, hammer, ruler, pencil, window, cement, rake, garden, cable, paintbrush, painter, gloves, ruler, monkey, juice, library, mall, city, calendar, table, door, television, lamp, George, woman, mountain, school, water, rice, bouquet, bottle

Page 12

1. Proper noun
2. Common noun
3. Common noun
4. Common noun
5. Common noun
6. Proper noun
7. Common noun
8. Common noun
9. Common noun
10. Common noun

Page 13

1. Big Motors- proper noun
2. people and vehicles- common noun
3. Mr Peter - proper noun, truck.
4. brother and motorcycle- common noun
5. woman and van- common noun
6. grocer, car, city - common noun
7. salespersons and customers - common noun
8. car - common noun
9. farmer , truck, farm - common noun
10. buyer - common noun

Answer Key

Page 14

1. It was very hot on Sunday afternoon.
2. Mac and Kiara sat on the garden bench.
3. Mac was munching on chocolate cookies.
4. Kiara was looking at the garden weeds.
5. Mac put his cookie on the bench and joined her.
6. A group of ants swarmed around the cookies!
7. Mac was amazed to see the tiny creatures together.
8. Kiara ran inside and got a magnifying glass.
9. The children saw how the ants worked together.
10. Mac and Kiara saw more ants every evening.

Page 15

happiness

strength

friendship

love

wish

fragrance

speed

Children will make sentences on their own.

Page 16

1. A class of students.
2. An army of soldiers.
3. A crew of sailors.
4. A band of musicians.
5. A haul of fish.
6. A parliament of owls
7. A team of players.
8. A bouquet of flowers.
9. A bowl of rice.
10. A pack of cards.

Page 17

Patrick's cap

Pasty's mittens

Polly's ear plugs

Paula's scarf

Percy's jacket

Pablo's ice skates

Penny's gloves

Pam's socks

Page 18

1. Martha's
2. Earth's
3. planets'
4. orbits'
5. comet's
6. children's
7. Sun's
8. Jupiter's
9. Saturn's
10. Moon's

Page 19

1. like
2. celebrate
3. gets, goes, cooks
4. takes, uses
5. carves
6. cut, heat
7. eat
8. loves
9. eats
10. enjoys

Page 20

1. go
2. want
3. comes
4. picks, gives
5. see
6. collect
7. finds
8. work

Page 21

1. reached
2. placed
3. picked
4. filled
5. stacked
6. formed
7. shaped
8. liked
9. splashed
10. played

Page 22

planned

hurried

moved

tried

liked

jumped

played

laughed

stopped

hopped

Answer key

Page 23

1. visited
2. helped
3. followed
4. practiced
5. rolled
6. aimed
7. hit
8. talked
9. guided
10. bowled

Page 24

said
saw
told
left
brought
stood
ran
felt
thought
understood

Page 25

1. flapped, turned
2. drifted, landed
3. jumped, picked, swallowed
4. found
5. poked, pulled, ripped
6. flew

Page 26

1. will climb
2. will buy
3. will use
4. will need
5. will also
6. will help
7. will tell
8. will have

Page 27

1. will go
2. will pack
3. will lack
4. will reach
5. will locate
6. will need
7. will show
8. will check
9. will leave
10. will board

Page 28

1. is
2. are
3. are
4. am
5. are
6. does
7. does
8. have
9. has
10. have

Page 29

1. did
2. was
3. did
4. were
5. had
6. was
7. were
8. was